Laugh And Grow Wise

Griffith And Parran Publisher

In the interest of creating a more extensive selection of rare historical book reprints, we have chosen to reproduce this title even though it may possibly have occasional imperfections such as missing and blurred pages, missing text, poor pictures, markings, dark backgrounds and other reproduction issues beyond our control. Because this work is culturally important, we have made it available as a part of our commitment to protecting, preserving and promoting the world's literature. Thank you for your understanding.

CONTENTS.

CRUEL JACK.

CHERRY PIE.

FRED AND HIS SHADOW.

MIND THE BULL.

THE TRAGICAL END OF WILFUL TOMMY.

MEDDLESOME MAT.

GREEDY BOB.

CRUEL JACK.

Said Jacky to mamma one day,
   "Do let me take my hat,
"And go out to the fields to play
   "With old black Tom the cat."

Mamma said, "Yes, but take great care,
   "The cat you know has claws;
"You must not pull him by the hair,
   "Nor make him wet his paws."

Thought Jack, "What fun 'twill be to see
   "Old Tommy try to scratch,
"And as I'm thrice as big as he,
   "I shall be quite his match."

He tied him with a piece of cord,
   And took the watering pan,
Then all the water on him poured,
   And laughing, round him ran.

And then he pulled his fur and tail,* * * *
　* * * The cat began to grow,
And Jack began to get quite pale,
　And shook from head to toe.

Bigger and bigger grew the cat,
　Till, thrice as big as Jack,
He seized him as he would a rat,
　And scratched his face and back.

Then in his mouth he took him up,
　And carried him away;
But whether on him he did sup
　I really cannot say.

CHERRY PIE.

THREE little girls sat down to eat
   A hearty dinner one fine day;
And Sally brought some bread and meat,
   And a great pie upon a tray.

"Oh, what is in that pie, I wonder?"
   Said Mary, when she saw the crust,—
"Oh, how I wish I might look under;
   "Do, Sally, cut it, or I must!"

Now Caroline and Susan sit
   As quiet as two little mice;
Says Sally, "Ere I open it
   "I tell you they are cherries nice.

"But children, eat them carefully,
   "Swallow the crust and fruit alone;
"You know not what the end may be
   "Of swallowing one single stone."

So Caroline and Susan eat
   As carefully as they were able,
While Mary, who loved all things sweet,
   Left not one stone upon the table.

"Oh, Mary! you will rue this sadly!"
   Cried Sally, as they went to play—
They played, and Mary felt quite badly
   Towards the evening of that day.

And all that night much worse grew she,
    And when the morning sun came out,
There was a little cherry tree
    That in poor Mary's mouth did sprout.

Now 'mid the boughs a fairy stood,
    Who thus to the three children said:
"Here, Caroline and Susan good,
    "Come to your Sister Mary's bed.

"Obedient girls and boys may share
    "What cherries on these boughs may be,
"But Mary in her mouth must bear,
    "Long as she lives her cherry tree!"

Poor Mary cried—her flood of tears,
    But made the tree grow faster there;
When next you eat a pie, my dears,
    Of Mary's cherry tree beware!

FRED AND HIS SHADOW.

I will tell you a story of cowardly Fred,
   Who was always so frightened at night;
Because it was dark when he went to bed,
   And he could not sleep without light.

So he begged his mamma to go and buy
   For him a candle thick;
And he promised that he no more would cry,
   When he looked at the blazing wick.

But he awoke up in the night,
   And then he thought he saw
Upon the wall a dreadful sight,
   A black man with a paw!

He shook with fright, and it moved too!
   He leapt quite out of bed;
The great black man still bigger grew,
   And followed silly Fred.

He ran quite quickly through the door.
　　The black man disappeared!

*　　*　　*　　*　　*　　*　　*

So fast did he run, that he tumbled down
　　The stairs which he quite forgot;
He tumbled down and broke his crown,
　　And lay there like a shot.

Then on the mat he lay forlorn,
　　Till Betty brought her tray;
Till Betty came at peep of dawn,
　　And threw poor Fred away.

MIND THE BULL.

"Listen Neddy, well to me,
"There a savage bull you see,
"Neither you nor Polly may
"In the field nor near him play."
So both Ned and Polly cried
"Yes, papa!" and off they hied,
Many pretty flowers to pull,
And quite forgot about the bull.
"Oh!" said they, "how near we are!
"Where, I wonder, is papa?"
"Look how still bull stands," says Ned;
"He does not even move his head.

"What flower just behind him grows?
"A blue-bell, buttercup, or rose?
"To gather it I think I dare,
"And I am sure the bull won't care."
So right into the field they go,
Gently creeping on tiptoe.........
First to bellow he began,
Then at the children fast he ran,
And tossed them up so high that soon
He left them hanging on the moon.

THE TRAGICAL END OF WILFUL TOMMY.

Papa and mamma for a walk were gone out,
    And granny sat reading her book,
When Tommy her grandson—a lad short and stout—
    Chanced out of the window to look.

"Oh granny! it's raining so hard, I declare!
    "I should so like to go and get wet."
"No Tom! stay at home," says granny, "take care
    "Lest more than you wish for you get."

But Tom would not listen to granny's advice,
    Nor take a great coat or umbrella;
Then out of the house he ran off in a trice,
    But he'll pay for it, poor little fellow.

Awhile he kept running, and thought it so nice
    And cool to be wet to the skin;
But soon he got tired, and the rain was like ice,
    As it fell on his nose and his chin.

He stood shaking and quaking, and sad to relate
   (As granny so truly did say),
Stout Tommy was waiting a terrible fate,—
   He felt himself melting away!

Tommy tried to run home, but could not stir a peg,
   Oh what is poor Tommy to do!
See his head, his straw hat, and each arm, and each leg,
   How thinner and thinner they grew.

The policeman comes by at the very next minute,
   But nothing to Tommy did say;
A stick lay in a puddle, and Tommy was in it,
   For Tommy had melted away.

His parents came home, they had wrapped themselves well
   In coats, cloaks, capes, kerchiefs, and plaid;
But Tommy! his fate to each other they tell,
   How it happened as granny had said.

MEDDLESOME MAT.

MEDDLESOME Matthew fancied he had
    Eyes at his fingers' end,
Till his experience painful and sad,
    Taught him his manners to mend.

Once in a box some "goodies" he spied,
    In his fingers, as usual, went,
Vainly to move them Meddlesome tried,
    For the "goody" was Roman cement.

Then comes the mason, angry and hot,
    Looking as black as thunder,
And having Matthew a prisoner got,
    Threatens to saw him asunder.

Once in a jar determined to look,
    Full of some grease of a bear,
Fingers the usual liberty took,
    But he pulled them out covered with hair.

"Take your hands from your pockets; why where
    have you been?"
    Cries dad when his fingers appeared.
"Meddling again, that is easily seen,
    "For your fingers have each got a beard."

A basket once came, of a curious make,
    Matthew saw something was in it;
So he put in his hands just to give it a shake,
    But pulled them out quick the next minute.

And look at the end of each finger-end dangles
    A crab with its sharp little claws,
Which Meddlesome Matthew's ten finger-ends mangles
    Oh see how he dances and roars.

Still the crabs dangle, still the crabs squeeze,
    And blood at each finger-end comes;
Matthew now no more fancies he sees
    With either his fingers or thumbs.

GREEDY BOB.

ALL the other schoolboys good,
   When their parents sent a cake,
Cut it all up, as they should,
   That each boy a piece might take.

Greedy Bob devoured it all,
   And would not give one bit away;
So instead of growing tall
   He got shorter every day.

Bob became so ill at last,
   His cakes he could no longer eat,
So in a box he locked them fast,
   To keep them for a future treat.

The rats and mice soon found the box,
   And smelt out Bobby's sugary hoard,
They little cared for keys or locks,
   And quickly through the box they gnawed

Now Bobby brought a cake one day,
    Unlocked the cake box in a trice;
No cakes he found, but strange to say,
    The box was full of rats and mice.

Then loud they squealed, as all jumped up,
    "Here's Bobby with another cake!
"On Bob himself we now will sup,
    "And a rare supper we will make!"

Bob seized his cake, the rats ran after,
    And all the schoolboys followed fast,
And Bob amid their shouts of laughter,
    Fell headlong in a pond at last.

Finis.